The North and the South

by Margaret McNamara

Table of Contents

Introduction 2
Chapter 1 What Was the Civil War? 4
Chapter 2 What Was the South Like? 8
Chapter 3 What Was the North Like? 12
Chapter 4 Why Did the Civil War Happen? ... 16
Summary 20
Glossary 22
Index 24

Introduction

What was **the Civil War**? What was **the North**? What was **the South**? Read to learn the answers.

▲ The Civil War had many battles.

Words to Know

 Abraham Lincoln

 plantations

 seceded

 slavery

 territories

 the Civil War

 the North

 the South

See the Glossary on page 22.

Chapter 1

What Was the Civil War?

The Civil War was a United States war. The war was between the states. The North fought the South.

The North and the South

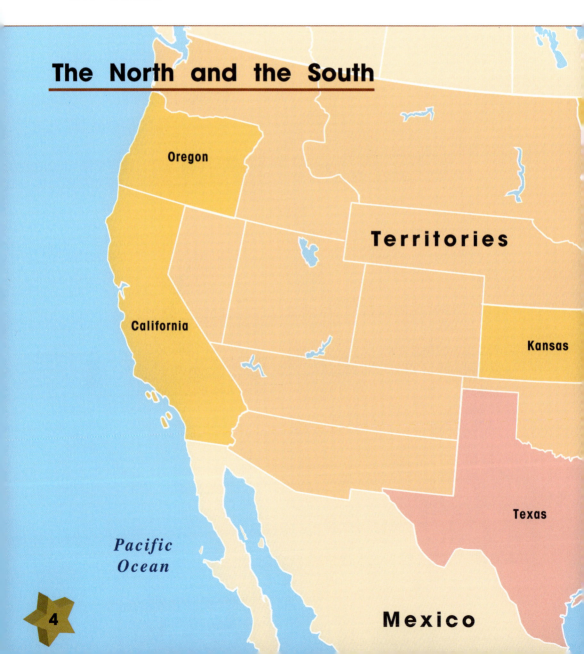

The North was the Northern states. The South was the Southern states.

Chapter 1

The Civil War had many battles. Many battles were in the South. Some battles were in the North.

▲ This battle was in the South.

What Was the Civil War?

The Civil War started in 1861. The Civil War ended in 1865. The North won the Civil War.

▲ General Grant   ▲ General Lee

Did You Know?

General Grant led the Northern army. General Lee led the Southern army.

Chapter 2

What Was the South Like?

The South had big farms. The farms were **plantations**. Cotton grew on many plantations.

▲ This plantation was in the South.

Did You Know?

Cotton is a plant. People make clothes from cotton.

The South had **slavery**. Slaves worked on the plantations. Slaves picked the cotton. Slaves cleaned the cotton.

It's a Fact

Slaves were not free. Other people owned the slaves.

▲ Slaves worked on this plantation.

Chapter 2

Slaves lived on the plantations. Slaves lived in small houses. The small houses were cabins.

▲ Slaves lived in these cabins.

What Was the South Like?

Other people owned the plantations. These people lived on the plantations. These people lived in large houses.

▲ This large house was on a plantation.

Chapter 3

What Was the North Like?

The North had factories. People worked in the factories. People made many things in factories.

▲ This factory was in Massachusetts.

The North had many big cities. People lived in the big cities. Factories were in the big cities.

▲ Philadelphia was a city in Pennsylvania.

Chapter 3

The North had railroads. People traveled on the railroads.

▲ This railroad was in New York.

What Was the North Like?

The North did not want slavery. Some Northern people helped slaves.

▲ Some Northern people helped slaves escape.

People to Know

Harriet Beecher Stowe wrote a book. The book was about slavery. Many people read the book.

▲ Harriet Beecher Stowe

▲ Harriet Beecher Stowe wrote this book.

Chapter 4

Why Did the Civil War Happen?

The Civil War happened because of slavery. The United States had **territories**. The South wanted slavery in the territories. The North did not want slavery.

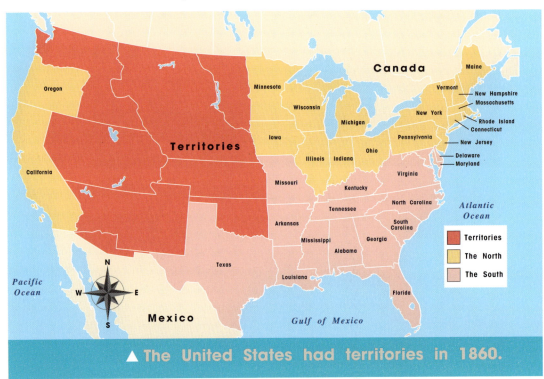

▲ The United States had territories in 1860.

Solve This

Look at the map. How many states had slavery? How many states did not have slavery? How many states were in the United States?

Answers: Fifteen states had slavery. Eighteen states did not have slavery. Thirty-three states were in the United States.

Abraham Lincoln became president. Abraham Lincoln became president in 1861. Lincoln did not want slavery in the territories. The South was angry.

▲ Lincoln became president of the United States.

Chapter 4

Seven Southern states **seceded**. The states started a new country. Later, four more Southern states seceded.

▲ The new country was in the South.

Why Did the Civil War Happen?

The new country had soldiers. The North had soldiers. The soldiers fought at Fort Sumter. The Civil War started.

▲ The Civil War started at Fort Sumter.

Then and Now

Soldiers used Fort Sumter.
Now tourists visit Fort Sumter.

Summary

The South had slavery. The North did not want slavery. Southern states started a new country. The Civil War started.

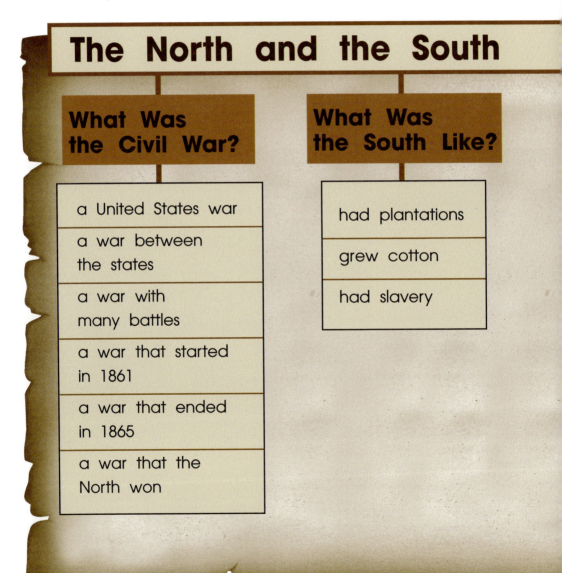

The North and the South

What Was the Civil War?	What Was the South Like?
a United States war	had plantations
a war between the states	grew cotton
a war with many battles	had slavery
a war that started in 1861	
a war that ended in 1865	
a war that the North won	

What Was the North Like?	Why Did the Civil War Happen?
had factories	because of slavery
had big cities	The South wanted slavery in territories.
had railroads	The North did not want slavery in territories.
	President Lincoln did not want slavery in territories.
	Southern states seceded.
	Southern states started a new country.

Think About It

1. What was the South like?
2. What was the North like?
3. Why did the Civil War happen?

Glossary

Abraham Lincoln a president of the United States

Abraham Lincoln became president in 1861.

plantations big farms

*Slaves worked on the **plantations**.*

seceded left the country

*Seven Southern states **seceded**.*

slavery people owning other people

*The South had **slavery**.*

territories land owned by a country

The United States had **territories**.

the Civil War a war between the states

The Civil War started in 1861.

the North the Northern states

The North had many big cities.

the South the Southern states

The South wanted slavery in the territories.

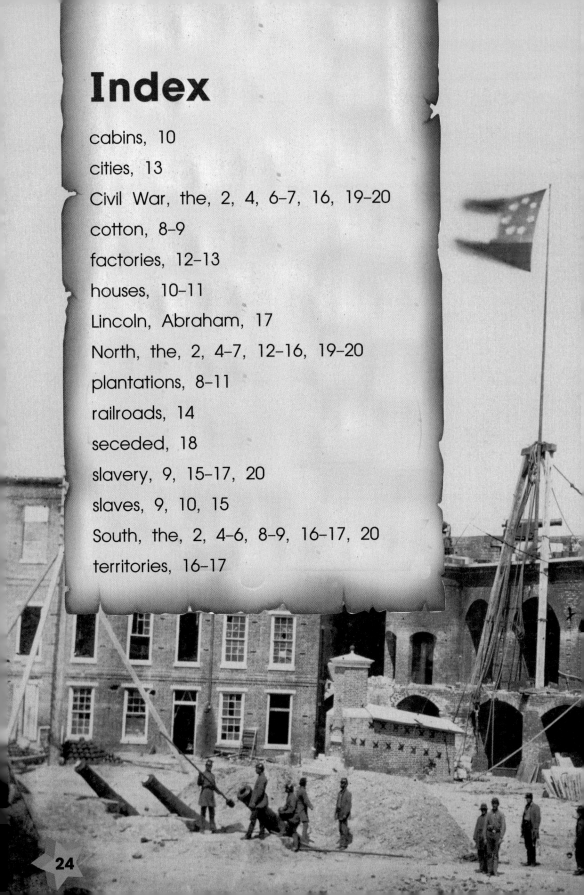

Index

cabins, 10

cities, 13

Civil War, the, 2, 4, 6–7, 16, 19–20

cotton, 8–9

factories, 12–13

houses, 10–11

Lincoln, Abraham, 17

North, the, 2, 4–7, 12–16, 19–20

plantations, 8–11

railroads, 14

seceded, 18

slavery, 9, 15–17, 20

slaves, 9, 10, 15

South, the, 2, 4–6, 8–9, 16–17, 20

territories, 16–17